Tell Me Why

WHY?

I Burp

Katie Marsico

Published in the United States of America by Cherry Lake Publishing
Ann Arbor, Michigan
www.cherrylakepublishing.com

Content Adviser: Lisa K. Militello, PhD, MPH, CPNP, The Ohio State University
Reading Adviser: Marla Conn, ReadAbility, Inc.

Photo Credits: © bonzodog/Shutterstock Images, cover, 1, 11; © Samuel Borges Photography/
Shutterstock Images, cover, 1, 9; © rmnoa357/Shutterstock Images, cover, 1, 17; © Isuaneye/Shutterstock
Images, cover, 1, 5; © SimonDGCrinks/iStock cover, 1; © RapidEye/iStock, cover, 1, 13;
© Laboko/Shutterstock Images, 7; © Anneka /Shutterstock Images, 9; © Flashon Studio/Shutterstock
Images, 11; © Flashon Studio/Shutterstock Images, 15; © La Gorda/Shutterstock Images, 17;
© pedalist/Shutterstock Images, 19; © Monkey Business Images/Shutterstock Images, 21;

Library of Congress Cataloging-in-Publication Data

Marsico, Katie, 1980- author.
 I burp / by Katie Marsico.
    pages cm. -- (Tell me why)
 Summary: "Young children are naturally curious about themselves. Tell Me
Why I Burp offers answers to their most compelling questions about their
rumbling tummy. Age-appropriate explanations and appealing photos encourage
readers to continue their quest for knowledge. Additional text features and
search tools, including a glossary and an index, help students locate
information and learn new words."—Provided by publisher.
 Audience: Ages 6-10.
 Audience: K to grade 3.
 Includes bibliographical references and index.
 ISBN 978-1-63188-992-9 (hardcover) -- ISBN 978-1-63362-031-5 (pbk.) --
ISBN 978-1-63362-070-4 (pdf) -- ISBN 978-1-63362-109-1 (ebook) 1.
Belching--Juvenile literature. 2. Digestion--Juvenile literature. 3. Human
physiology--Juvenile literature. I. Title.

QP145.M3677 2015
612.3'2--dc23

2014025719

Cherry Lake Publishing would like to acknowledge the work of The Partnership for 21st Century Skills.
Please visit www.21.org for more information.

Printed in the United States of America
Corporate Graphics

Table of Contents

About to Explode?

Is Tasha about to explode? She and her mom just ate lunch. Their pizza was delicious, but now Tasha is full. In fact, she feels like a giant bubble is trapped inside her.

Without warning, the feeling spreads upward. Tasha makes a croaking, rumbling sound. She isn't turning into a frog or a car engine. She's burping! After excusing herself, Tasha wonders aloud what is causing the burp to form inside her.

You might burp after eating a big meal, such as pizza.

Tasha's mom explains that burping, or belching, is a **physical** process. It is the body's way of releasing gases. These gases sometimes become trapped in a person's digestive system. The digestive system is the group of **organs** and **glands** that break down food into **nutrients** and waste.

Some foods, like onions, can make you burp more than others.

There are many reasons why extra gases build up in the digestive system. Most involve swallowing air. People swallow air when they eat, drink, use a straw, chew gum, or suck on candy.

Drinking soda and other **carbonated** beverages can lead to trapped gases, too. So does eating certain foods or not digesting food properly.

Are you able to guess why carbonated beverages make you burp? Do you think it has anything to do with the bubbles in these drinks?

Drinking soda can make you burp.

An Escape Route

Tasha is embarrassed that she burped so loudly. On the other hand, she's also relieved. Her stomach doesn't feel like it's about to pop anymore!

Tasha's mom reminds her that burping is normal. She says that everyone belches from time to time. Without burping, gases often remain trapped in a person's digestive system. This leads to feelings of **bloating**.

ASK QUESTIONS!

Why do babies need to be burped so often?
Ask someone you know, visit the library, or go on-line with an adult to find the answer.

Babies need to be burped after eating.

Burping provides trapped gases with an escape **route.** That path winds upward through the digestive system.

When gases build up, they stretch the stomach. This causes a person's esophagus muscles to relax. The esophagus is a muscular tube. It reaches between the mouth and the stomach. Trapped gases that rush up the esophagus escape through the mouth.

Sometimes burps come out accidentally.

Sounds and Smells

Tasha now understands how and why she burps. Yet she still wonders why belching is so loud. Sometimes burps smell, too.

Tasha's mom tells her that the noise is created by gases moving through the digestive system. As they rush toward the mouth, they cause loose **tissue** near the upper esophagus to **vibrate**. These vibrations are what make the croaking, rumbling sound Tasha heard.

Some spices can cause burps to smell.

When burps have an **odor**, it's usually because of something a person recently ate. Food often shares the same space as the trapped gases, so it affects their odor. Gases that don't move all the way down the esophagus usually don't lead to smelly burps.

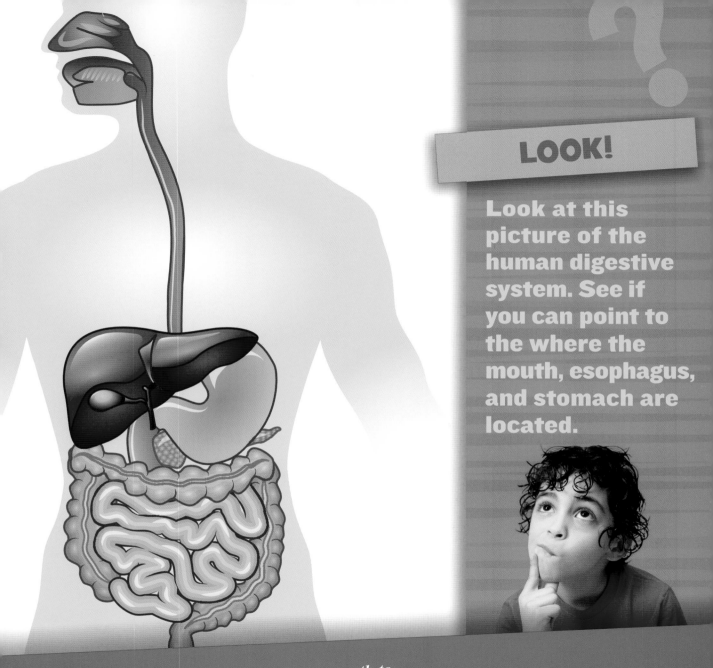

Your esophagus is what connects your mouth to your stomach.

How to Handle Burping

Tasha now knows that it's impossible to totally avoid burping. It would be unhealthy, too. Still, her mom says there are a few tricks people use to reduce belching. Eating and drinking slowly often helps because it prevents **indigestion**. Cutting out or limiting carbonated beverages tends to work, too.

Eating and drinking slowly can help reduce burping.

What about those times when a burp is beyond Tasha's control? People should always try to cover their mouth if they think they're about to burp. Saying "excuse me" or "pardon me" after belching is polite, too. These tips help Tasha understand her body better. Now she won't worry about bottling up her burp. Instead, she can focus on enjoying her dinner.

Practicing good manners can help you deal with burping at the dinner table.

Think About It

In countries such as Bahrain, many people believe burping after a meal is good manners. They consider a belch a compliment to the person who prepared the food. Why do you think burping is sometimes viewed this way?

People aren't the only living creatures to burp. Animals do, too! In fact, scientists say that cows' belches actually add to environmental pollution. Why do you think this is the case?

Can you think of another way that trapped gases are released from the digestive system? How is it similar to burping? How is it different?

Glossary

bloating (BLOW-ting) an often uncomfortable condition that occurs when fluids or gases cause something to swell

carbonated (KAR-buh-nayte-uhd) containing dissolved carbon dioxide

glands (GLANDZ) organs that produce substances used by the body

indigestion (in-di-JES-chuhn) discomfort in the stomach or chest caused by difficulty digesting food

nutrients (NU-tree-uhntz) substances that living things need to grow and stay healthy

odor (OH-duhr) a frequently strong, distinctive smell

organs (OR-guhnz) body parts such as the stomach that perform a specific job

physical (FIZ-uh-kuhl) to do with the body

route (ROWT) a path that features starting and end points

tissue (TIH-shoo) a material that forms the body parts of living things

vibrate (VYE-brayte) to move back and forth or from side to side using short, quick movements

Find Out More

Books:

Bennett, Artie, and Pranas T. Naujokaitis (illustrator). *Belches, Burps, and Farts, Oh My!* Maplewood, NJ: Blue Apple Books, 2014.

Johnson, Rebecca L. *Your Digestive System.* Minneapolis: Lerner Publishing Group, 2013.

Kolpin, Molly. *Why Do I Burp?* North Mankato, MN: Capstone Press, 2015.

Web Sites:

KidsHealth—Why Do I Burp?
http://kidshealth.org/kid/talk/yucky/burp.html
Learn more about how and why people burp.

Kidzworld—The Ins and Outs of Burping
www.kidzworld.com/article/756-the-ins-and-outs-of-burping
Enjoy an article and fun facts about belching!

Index

About the Author

Katie Marsico is the author of more than 150 children's books. She lives in a suburb of Chicago, Illinois, with her husband and children.